Public Library District of Columbia

Our Community Helpers

Nurses
Help

by Dee Ready

Consulting editor: Gail Saunders-Smith, PhD

D1532198

CAPSTONE PRESS
a capstone imprint

Pebble Books are published by Capstone Press,
1710 Roe Crest Drive, North Mankato, Minnesota 56003
www.capstonepub.com

Copyright © 2013 by Capstone Press, a Capstone imprint. All rights reserved.
No part of this publication may be reproduced in whole or in part, or stored in a
retrieval system, or transmitted in any form or by any means, electronic, mechanical,
photocopying, recording, or otherwise, without written permission of the publisher.

Library of Congress Cataloging-in-Publication Data
Cataloging-in-Publication information is on file with the Library of Congress.
ISBN: 978-1-62065-080-6 (library binding)
ISBN: 978-1-62065-849-9 (paperback)
ISBN: 978-1-4765-1720-9 (ebook PDF)

Note to Parents and Teachers

The Our Community Helpers set supports national social studies
standards for how groups and institutions work to meet individual
needs. This book describes and illustrates nurses. The images
support early readers in understanding the text. The repetition of
words and phrases helps early readers learn new words. This book
also introduces early readers to subject-specific vocabulary words,
which are defined in the Glossary section. Early readers may need
assistance to read some words and to use the Table of Contents,
Glossary, Read More, Internet Sites, and Index sections of the book.

Printed in the United States of America in North Mankato, Minnesota.
012015   008670R

Table of Contents

What Is a Nurse? 5

Where Nurses Work 7

What Nurses Do 11

Clothes and Tools 15

Nurses Help. 21

Glossary 22

Read More 23

Internet Sites. 23

Index 24

What Is a Nurse?

Nurses care for people who are sick or hurt. They also help healthy people stay healthy. Nurses usually work with doctors.

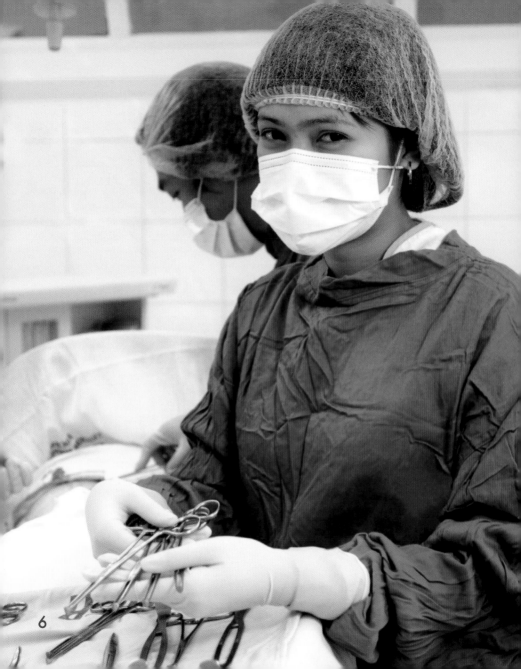

Where Nurses Work

Most nurses work in hospitals or clinics. They often work with certain kinds of patients. Some work only with children or with people having surgery.

Some nurses work other places. They may work in schools or nursing homes. Others may visit patients in their homes.

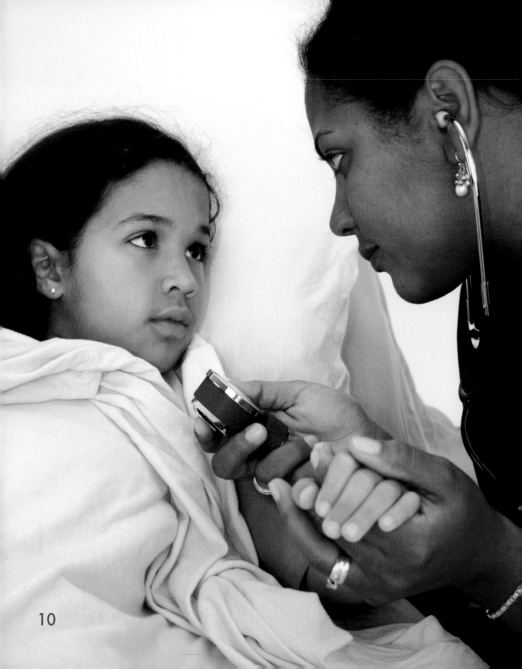

What Nurses Do

Nurses help people who are sick or hurt. They give patients medicine. They clean wounds. They try to make patients comfortable.

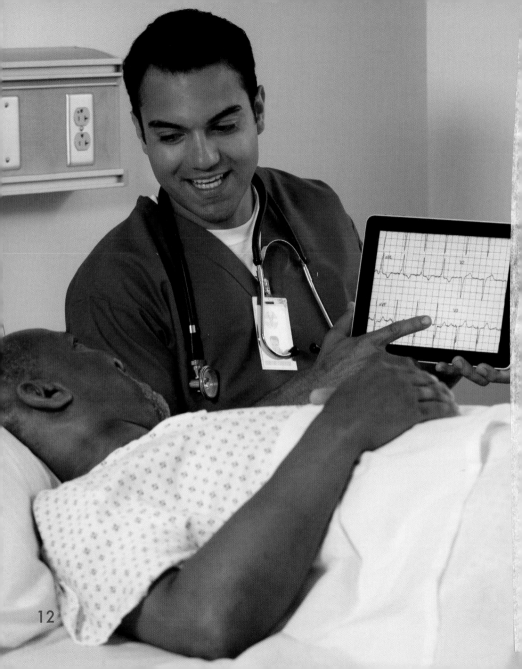

Nurses help people stay well. They give shots to prevent diseases. They teach people about eating well, exercise, and other health topics.

Clothes and Tools

Nurses usually wear loose shirts and pants called scrubs. Gloves protect nurses and patients from germs.

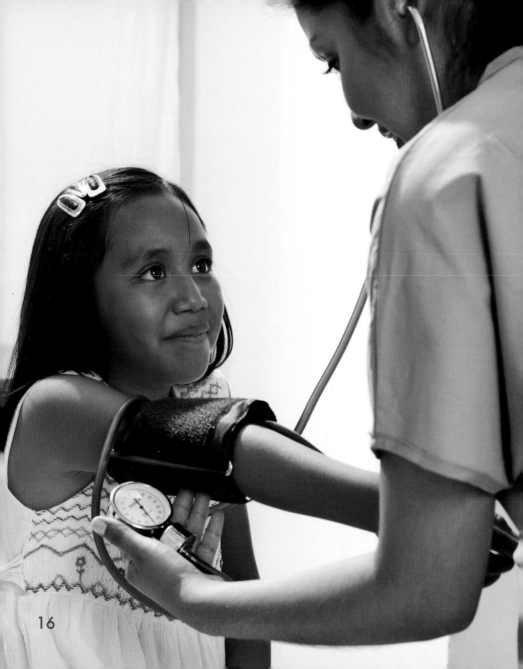

Nurses gather information with tools. They measure blood pressure with a cuff. They measure temperature with a thermometer.

Nurses use stethoscopes to hear heartbeats and breathing. They put all of the information in a patient's chart.

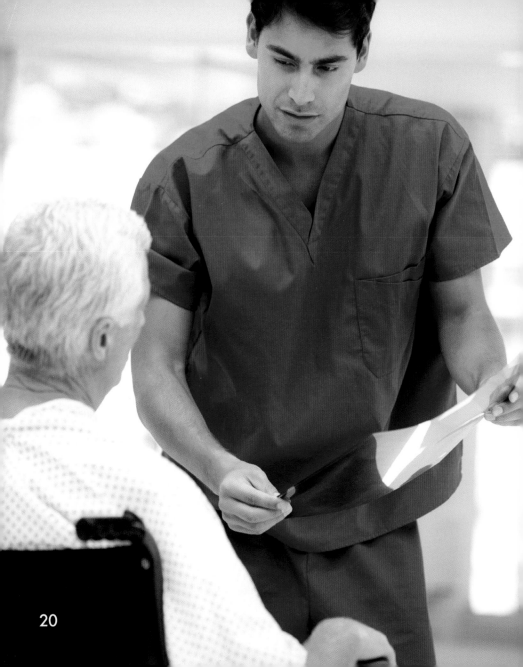

Nurses Help

Nurses help the community.
They help people feel better.
Nurses want their patients
to be happy and healthy.

Glossary

blood pressure—the force of blood as it flows through a person's body

chart—a record of medical information about a patient

cuff—a band that can be filled with air and wrapped around an arm to control blood flow when measuring blood pressure

germ—a tiny living thing that can cause illness

nursing home—a place where people who cannot care for themselves get personal and medical care

patient—a person who gets medical care

stethoscope—a tool used to listen to the heart and lungs

surgery—an operation that involves cutting into the body to remove or fix a part of the body

wound—an injury or cut

Read More

Macken, JoAnn Early. *Nurses.* People in My Community. New York: Gareth Stevens Pub., 2011.

Murray, Julie. *Nurses.* Going to Work. Edina, Minn.: ABDO, 2011.

Zeiger, Jennifer. *What Do They Do? Nurses.* Community Connections. Ann Arbor, Mich.: Cherry Lake Pub., 2010.

Internet Sites

FactHound offers a safe, fun way to find Internet sites related to this book. All of the sites on FactHound have been researched by our staff.

Here's all you do:

Visit *www.facthound.com*

Type in this code: 9781620650806

Super-cool stuff! Check out projects, games and lots more at
www.capstonekids.com

Index

charts, 19
children, 7
clinics, 7
clothing, 15
cuffs, blood pressure, 17,
doctors, 5
germs, 15
home care, 9
hospitals, 7
medicine, 11

nursing homes, 9
rubber gloves, 15
schools, 9
scrubs, 15
shots, 13
stethoscopes, 19
surgery, 7
teaching, 13
thermometers, 17
tools, 17

Word Count: 179
Grade: 1
Early-Intervention Level: 18

Editorial Credits
Gillia Olson, editor; Gene Bentdahl, designer; Eric Manske, production specialist

Photo Credits
Capstone Studio: Karon Dubke, cover; Corbis: Ann Summa, 16; Getty Images: Blend Images/Ariel Skelley, 12; Newscom: Tetra Images, 8; Shutterstock: forestpath, 18, Jeff Banke, 14, maska, 6, Monkey Business Images, 20, Rob Marmion, 4, 10